SCHOOL BUS

BY ALEX SUMMERS

Rourke
Educational Media
rourkeeducationalmedia.com

Before & After Reading Activities

Teaching Focus:
Concepts of Print: Have students find capital letters and punctuation in a sentence. Ask students to explain the purpose for using them in a sentence.

Before Reading:

Building Academic Vocabulary and Background Knowledge

Before reading a book, it is important to set the stage for your child or student by using pre-reading strategies. This will help them develop their vocabulary, increase their reading comprehension, and make connections across the curriculum.

1. Read the title and look at the cover. *Let's make predictions about what this book will be about.*
2. Take a picture walk by talking about the pictures/photographs in the book. Implant the vocabulary as you take the picture walk. Be sure to talk about the text features such as headings, the Table of Contents, glossary, bolded words, captions, charts/diagrams, or Index.
3. Have students read the first page of text with you then have students read the remaining text.
4. Strategy Talk – use to assist students while reading.
   - Get your mouth ready
   - Look at the picture
   - Think…does it make sense
   - Think…does it look right
   - Think…does it sound right
   - Chunk it – by looking for a part you know
5. Read it again.

Content Area Vocabulary
Use glossary words in a sentence.

bright
bus
climb
rows

After Reading:

Comprehension and Extension Activity

After reading the book, work on the following questions with your child or students in order to check their level of reading comprehension and content mastery.

1. *Why does the main character ride the bus? (Summarize)*
2. *How many windows are on a school bus? (Asking Questions)*
3. *Have you ridden a school bus? What was it like? (Text to self connection)*
4. *When the bus stops to pick up children, what must the traffic do? (Asking Questions)*

Extension Activity

Make Your Own Bus! Have an adult draw a template of the body of a school bus. Trace it onto a piece of yellow construction paper. Cut it out with scissors. Then cut circles for the wheels out of black construction paper. Glue them on to your bus and color in the windows and stop signs. Put the name of your school on the side of the bus. You can also add drawings of you and all your friends riding on the bus.

Table of Contents

Ready to Ride

Ready to go!
How will I get there?

I know! I will take
a school **bus**.

6

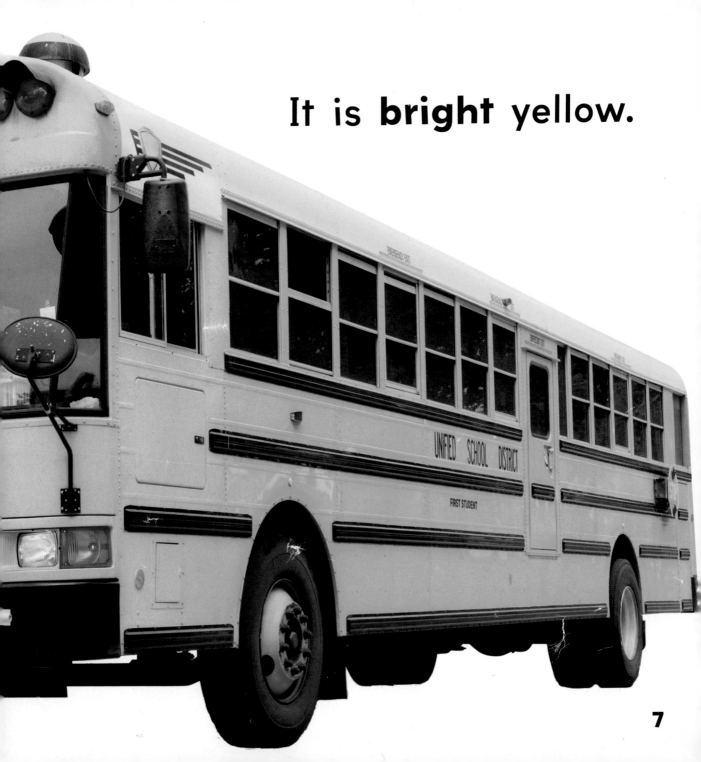

It is **bright** yellow.

The driver says, "Good Morning!"
I have to **climb** the bus's stairs.

bus driver

9

There are thirteen **rows** of seats. Each side has thirteen windows.

EMERGENCY DOOR
PORTE DE SECOURS

seat

Busy Bus

We stop to pick up other students. Stop signs come out on the sides of the bus.

stop sign

Cars stop to let everyone get on. The driver shuts the door.

We don't move until everyone sits down.

Buses at School

We pull in to school.
Other buses are there.

The bus gets me to school safely. The driver says, "Have a nice day!"

I climb down the stairs and am on my way.

stairs

22

Picture Glossary

 **bright** (brite): When something is a bright color, it is bold and easy to see.

 **bus** (buhs): A large vehicle for carrying people, usually following a specific route.

 **climb** (klime): When you climb something you move forward in an upward slope.

 **rows** (rohs): Rows are things, like seats, that are arranged in a straight line.

Index

Websites to Visit

www.mybusgames.com

www.playgamesward.com/busgames.html

www.primarygames.com

About the Author

Alex Summers enjoys all forms of transportation. Especially if they are taking her to places she has never been or seen before. She loves to travel, read, write, and dream about all the places she will visit someday!

Meet The Author!
www.meetREMauthors.com

Library of Congress PCN Data

School Bus / Alex Summers
(Transportation and Me!)
ISBN 978-1-68342-160-3 (hard cover)
ISBN 978-1-68342-202-0 (soft cover)
ISBN 978-1-68342-229-7 (e-Book)
Library of Congress Control Number: 2016956524

Rourke Educational Media
Printed in the United States of America,
North Mankato, Minnesota

Also Available as:

ROURKE'S
e-Books

© 2017 Rourke Educational Media

www.rourkeeducationalmedia.com

Edited by: Keli Sipperley
Cover design by: Tara Raymo
Interior design by: Rhea Magaro-Wallace
Photo Credits: Cover © matt_dela, Si_Gal, zagar; page 5 © MichaelJung, eyewave, tarasov_vl, Rouzes; page 6, 22 © MichaelJung; page 7 © narvikk; page 8 © monkeybusinessimages; page 11 © Diane Lambombarbe; page 12 © nmaxfield; page 13 © LaserLens; page 15 © Doug Cannell; page 17 © &#169morganl; page 21 © Christopher Futcher